Swayam Ganguly was born in Jamshedpur and currently resides in Kolkata. He wears many hats, being a published author, director of corporate films, and editorial consultant for various publishers. He has worked on biographies, mythology series, abridged versions of classics, encyclopedias, fact books, and written children's fiction.

# The Incredible Life of Mary Kom

## The Queen of Boxing

Swayam Ganguly

*Illustrations by*

*Mohit Suneja*

talking CUB

An Imprint of Speaking Tiger Books

TALKING CUB

Published by Speaking Tiger Books LLP

125A, Ground Floor, Shahpur Jat,

Near Asiad Village, New Delhi 110 049

First published in paperback in Talking Cub
by Speaking Tiger Books in 2024



ISBN: 978-93-5447-775-1

eISBN: 978-93-5447-897-0

10 9 8 7 6 5 4 3 2 1

Typeset in Georgia by Jojy Philip
Printed at HT Media Ltd, Greater Noida

To my late father R.G GANGULY

# Chapter One

The state of Manipur has produced renowned fighters right from mythological times. According to a legend in the Mahabharata, the third Pandava, Arjuna, visited Manipur. There he married the princess Chitrangada, who was a warrior too. They had a son, Babruvahana, who was trained in warfare from a young age.

The epic tells the story of how, after the Great War of the Mahabharata, the Pandavas performed the Ashwamedha Yajna. In this ceremony, the Ashwamedha horse was allowed to roam, and wherever it went became the territory of the one performing the ceremony. Arjuna was appointed the guardian of the Ashwamedha horse, and when the horse reached Manipur, it was captured by Babruvahana. A battle broke out between Manipur and the Pandava army, in which Babruvahana defeated the mighty Arjuna. In time, Babruvahana became the king of Manipur .

Manipur was a princely state before India's independence and became a part of India when the king signed an instrument of merger with India. Today, Manipur shares its boundaries with states like Nagaland, Mizoram and Assam on three sides, and is flanked by the Sagaing region of Myanmar on the remaining side. Imphal is the capital of Manipur as well as its largest city.

Several ancient Indian texts, including the Mahabharata, mention a variation of the modern sport of boxing called 'mushti-yuddha' or 'fighting with fists'. Manipur, with its record of producing great fighters, has also produced some of the best boxers of modern times, like Dingko Singh, Devendro Singh, Suranjoy Singh, Laishram Sarita Devi, and Sarjubala Devi to name a few.

But the name that tops the list of boxers is Mary Kom—the most successful boxer at the Women's World Boxing Championships with a record six gold medals in the event, and bronze medal-winning Olympic champion. She was the first Indian boxer to win a medal at the Women's World Boxing Championships with a silver medal in the light flyweight (48 kg) category at the inaugural edition. Mary Kom's phenomenal achievement can be gauged by the fact that to date, no male Indian boxer has won a gold medal at the World Championships.

Manipur is no stranger to women fighting for their rights. The famous activist Irom Sharmila went on a hunger strike for more than a decade, protesting army excesses. In 1939, Manipuri women launched 'Nupi Lan', an agitation against the oppressive policies of the then Manipuri ruler. In 2004, the women of Manipur protested the oppressive laws shielding the armed forces by stripping naked in front of an army barrack in Imphal.

The common thread running through all these stories of brave women of Manipur—including Mary Kom—is that of courage, resilience, and persistence.

Mary Kom's amazing journey began in the small village of Kangathei that has a population of around 250 people. Kangathei is a village of Koms, who are a Manipuri hill tribe. The Koms are a very small tribe, spread over fifty-seven villages across Manipur, and all the members of this tribe are Christians. In Kangathei, the Koms lived like one big family. The bare fields of the village were separated by bamboo plantations and there were banana and pomelo trees growing in abundance. Roosters perched on the walls and wild ducks quacked around the small houses.

There were forty-nine houses, most of them single-storey mud houses with a thatched or tin roof. The ones owned by the relatively rich villagers were painted blue or pink. Most of the villagers worked in the fields as cultivators or agricultural labourers. However, some served in the police force and some were engaged as teachers in schools located nearby. Their language is a Manipuri dialect known as 'Maiteilon'.

Kangathei has one primary school, and there is no hospital or dispensary. There is no public transport as well that crosses the village, and commuters who need to travel to the city have to walk a kilometre to reach Moirang town, which has the facilities that are lacking in Kangathei.

Moirang is an important town for various reasons. It is near the famous Loktak lake, which is the world's only floating lake, and also the origin of many Manipuri fables, folk tales, and local history. The famous Lai Haraoba festival of the Meitei community is celebrated here. Moirang is also a meeting place for all the Koms from the neighbouring villages. They gather here to sell vegetables or other agricultural produce and buy essential household items.

Mary was the eldest child of Mangte Tonpa Kom and Mangte Akham Kom. Her family was not rich, and they had to face many hardships. When Mary was in Class 3, she dropped out of school and started helping out in the domestic

chores. She worked in the fields, helping her father, who was a landless agricultural labourer. Thankfully, things at home got better soon, and Mary returned to school, which was almost a kilometre away from her village.

Mary played and fought with boys rather than girls in her younger years, which earned her the nickname 'Second Pasay' in the village. In the local language, 'pasay' means boy. This label annoyed Mary no end. She was a wiry yet strong girl with more bones than fat, ready to take on anyone in a fight.

In 1867, the Queensberry Rules were formulated by a Welshman, John Graham Chambers, to establish amateur boxing. These rules laid down a code of conduct for boxing. Till then, the sport had existed as a form of prizefighting without a fixed set of rules.

Amateur boxing made its debut at the 1904 Olympics in the USA. The first Indian boxer to win an Olympic medal was Vijender Singh. He won a bronze in the men's middleweight (75 kg) category at the 2008 Beijing Olympics.

Women's boxing was introduced in the Olympics in London 2012 and the legend Mary Kom received India's second Olympic boxing medal when she won a bronze in the flyweight (51 kg) category.

# *Chapter Two*

On 16 August 1991, Mary's village was in the news for the wrong reason. A nine-year-old Mary was in church along with almost everyone for the Sunday service. Just as the service ended, there was a resounding crash. Soon, policemen and other officials arrived in numerous vehicles to tiny Kangathei. An Indian Airlines Boeing aeroplane from Calcutta had crashed into the nearby Thangjing Ching mountain range because of bad weather, and there were no survivors!

Kangathei was the designated base camp for rescue operations, and locals, including Mary's father, were hired to recover the bodies. This was the first time Mary had seen an aeroplane, but the thrill was dimmed by the horror of the dead bodies recovered from the crash and kept in the village.

MESMERISING FACTS ABOUT MANIPUR

Manipur is called 'the jewel of India' because it is surrounded by nine hills with an oval-shaped valley at the centre—a natural jewel.

In the past, Manipur was known by different names like Mitei-Leibak, Sanna-Leibak, Poirei-Lam, and Tilli-Koktong.

Ningthou Kangba is considered to be the first and foremost king of Manipur.

Manipur is the birthplace of the sport of polo. It is known as 'Sagol Kangjei', which literally means 'hockey played from the horse'.

Manipur has the world's earliest known written Constitution in the Loyumba Shinyen Constitution (the Loiyumpa Silyel). It is a proto-constitution from 429 AD by King Naophangba. It got its final written form in 1100 AD by King Loyumba. That means this Constitution precedes the famous Magna Carta of England (1215 AD)!

Manipur boasts of the world's only floating national park in the Keibul Lamjao national park.

India's third longest epic poem is from Manipur. The epic of *Khamba Thoibi* has 39,000 lines.

Mary's first school was the Loktak Christian Model High School, which was run by a Presbyterian mission in Moirang. It was one of the best schools in Moirang, and Mary's father had set aside small sums of money from his meager earnings so that he could enroll his eldest daughter in a good school. What pride he felt when Mary was admitted to this school!

Sometimes, Mary's father could not pay the school fees on time, and this embarrassed the children greatly as they were not allowed to enter the class or sit for examinations if their school fees remained unpaid. Mary's mother tried her best to save them from these embarrassing experiences.

From an early age, Mary realized that their family was hard-up for money. She was an understanding child who never demanded anything of her parents. Even during Christmas, which was the only time the children got new clothes to wear, Mary always accepted what was given to her without creating any fuss. Her only preference was boyish clothes like jeans, T-shirts, and shorts.

In the Kom society in those days, boys were given preference over girls when it came to education while the girls were married off early. But Mary's father held different views and wanted his daughter to study and make a mark rather than sit at home waiting to be married off. It was Mary's father's farsightedness that made her an independent spirit.

Mary had a busy life apart from her studies, as she was her father's right-hand woman. Apart from ploughing the fields, her other duties in the fields included handling heavy farming tools, carrying bundles of rice saplings for planting, and later, carrying heavy sacks of rice. There would be leeches in the wet rice fields, and occasionally water snakes too. Mary would pull off the leeches with her bare hands, or knock out the snakes. She used this experience many years later at a boxing camp when her friends ran away on spotting a snake but Mary was not scared.

Not all the children in the village worked as hard as Mary and her siblings. Most of Mary's friends spent their free time playing, eating, or sleeping. But Mary's father had taught his children to work hard from an early age. With time, Mary could do jobs that even bigger and stronger boys struggled with. For example, ploughing the fields demanded great strength and skill as the bullocks were not easy to manage. When Mary drove the animals in the field with ease, the menfolk of the village would stand and gape in amazement.

Mary would also carry home the straw left over after harvesting, which would be stored as cattle-feed. She had to fetch water from a long distance as there was no potable water in the village. She also accompanied her father up the hills to collect firewood and to the lake to fish.

Her mother needed Mary's help too in cooking, washing, gardening, cleaning the house, and

several other odd jobs! Neither Mary nor her siblings ever complained about anything. There was simply no time for all that. Their parents toiled harder than anybody else they had seen and also made endless sacrifices.

All the hard work would prove beneficial to Mary when she would begin her boxing career. Her strength and stamina helped her to battle bigger and more powerful opponents in the ring.

In his youth, Mary's father had been the village wrestling champion. He gave up wrestling to support his family. Mary's mother was always working. She wove shawls that she sold to pay for her children's school fees. All the vegetables came from her kitchen garden, and the leftovers were sold in the market. So, even though Mary's family was poor, they never ate poorly.

Mary's father was also an expert fisherman. Sometimes, he left home at the crack of dawn to go fishing and hunting. Mary's mother packed the day's food for him. When he returned only after dark, the children crowded around him excitedly, eager to see what he had brought back. He was especially good at catching eels, which he spread out for display in the kitchen. The big eels were exchanged for rice as they fetched a good price. This caused the innocent children much sadness as they wondered why the big fish were always sent away while they could eat only the little ones.

Very few families owned television sets, and Mary and her siblings used to watch movies in their uncle's house sometimes. Mary loved the action-packed martial arts films of Bruce Lee, Jackie Chan, and Jet Li, and dreamed of becoming a fighter like Bruce Lee. She would practice her Bruce Lee kicks on a younger cousin.

During school holidays, Mary and her two siblings would accompany their father to climb the Ningthiching hills, eight kilometers away. As the kids waited at the foothills, their father would climb up and throw the firewood down the slope for them to catch. Once, when Mary had accompanied her father alone, she fell into a hole and lost consciousness while waiting for him. Her father was terribly worried and they left for home after attending to Mary's cuts and bruises. These early cuts and bruises prepared Mary for the many injuries sustained throughout her boxing career later.

Mary's younger brother and sister looked up to her and she was protective towards them. When a bully beat up her brother, and he came home crying, Mary decided to take matters into her own hands. She went and twisted the bully's ears so hard that he promised never to repeat his act.

At the annual games and sports meets held in her school, Mary participated in every individual athletic event and would bag the first prize in most of them. The lucrative prizes were household items like cups, plates, and tiffin-boxes that delighted Mary's family, especially her little brother as he could now carry a tiffin-box to school like his other friends.

Pocket money was an alien concept in the village, but Mary and her friends devised ways to make small amounts of money. They collected bottles, tins, and containers, and sold them to a hawker. Mary also picked wild fruits and vegetables to sell them. The small amounts she earned this way was used to buy textbooks, pencils and erasers.

Mary moved to St Xavier's School in Moirang after Class 6. The thing Mary loved best about her new school was its huge playground. Mary participated and excelled in sports in her new school as well. Her teachers were impressed and suggested a career in sports to her father. The principal told him that he could take Mary to the Sports Authority of India (SAI) in Imphal.

But Mary's father was in a quandary. Would he be able to afford this?

# Chapter Three

Despite all the hunting, fishing, and farming Mary's father did, and her mother's gardening and weaving, there wasn't enough money to feed the family and educate the children. So, there were times when Mary's father was forced to remain away from his family, in search of work.

He would work as a woodcutter in the jungles of Ukhrul or Ta-menglong, located more than a hundred kilometres from their village. He hired himself out as a contract labourer, and the work involved cutting down trees deep in the forest, and carrying them to the road ready for transportation. When he came home, Mary's father would narrate to his children how there was only one truck, aptly named Shaktiman, that could drive up those rough and rugged hills. Sometimes, depending on the load, the woodcutters loaded the wood on the truck and then travelled on it to the nearest town, and returned to the forest after depositing the wood.

It was a dangerous job, and Mary's father had several near-death experiences. Once, he fell from a high tree onto a thorn bush. There were cuts and bruises all over his body as the thorns pierced his skin. Mary's father had to simply pull out the thorns from his

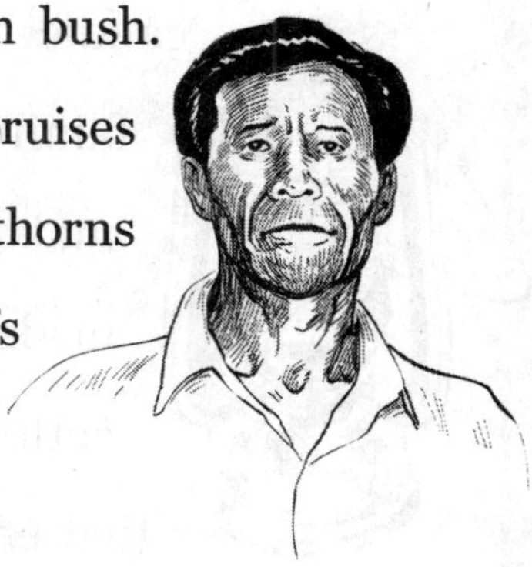

body himself, and wait for the wounds to heal. There were times when he had to spend the night in the forest, and he always slept in a half-sitting position then, so that he could get up and escape quickly in case an animal attacked him.

Mary's parents got to sit down to relax only for a while after dinner. Mary would be dead tired after dinner, but her father would ask her to roll out the mat and study as this was the only time for her to do her homework. Mary would sit and study by the light of a boton. Because

candles were expensive, Mary's family used these botons, or makeshift kerosene lamps made from used bottles and cotton wicks. They were not that effective as they emitted a lot of smoke and just a dim light, but they served the purpose. One boton sufficed for the entire house, which was just one room with an attached kitchen. Mary would finish her homework as fast as she could, read a few lessons, and then hit the bed. The moment her head touched the pillow, she was fast asleep.

As the days went by, Mary's father noticed and accepted her fierce passion for sport. He saved money to buy her a Captain bicycle, and Mary was elated. She rode with her friends and with her sister perched on the carrier at the back. She pretended she was riding a motorbike as she rode her bicycle on the village streets. One day, she pedaled so fast that her sister fell off. It was only after her friends yelled at her to stop did Mary discover that her sister was missing, and had to

cycle back quite a distance to pick her up.

Mary's father decided she should get sports training but without disturbing her education. He took her to a reputed athletics coach named Nipamacha Kunam. Mary was thrilled when he accepted her as his student. There were no admission fees or equipment charges, one only had to come early in the morning to exercise and train with the other athletes and have a balanced diet. The latter was a concern for Mary, and soon, the strain of cycling between Moirang and her village four times a day took a toll on her body. However, in that short stint, Mary picked up the right exercise techniques to build strength, stamina, and speed. She continued her exercises even after she stopped going to the centre.

Mary's teachers and friends constantly spoke of her zeal and talent for sports. This finally convinced her father that his daughter's future lay in sports and not academics He contacted his relatives in Imphal, and inquired if Mary could stay with them if an opportunity arose. This done, he began making inquiries about the Sports Authority of India (SAI) facility in Imphal. Finally, in 1999, a seventeen-year-old Mary left for Imphal to try her luck in getting admission at SAI Takyel.

*Nangnatouba, nangnaphangba*
*Einatouba, einaphangba.*

What you sow, you will reap

What I sow, I will reap.

These were the words Mary took with her to Imphal. Mary and her mother stayed in the house of her mother's nephew, Chungthang, who worked with Life Insurance Corporation. He introduced Mary to Coach Gosana of SAI, who was impressed with Mary's determination. He agreed to train Mary till her formal selection at SAI. Cousin Chungthang was a great help, advising Mary to choose an individual sport to better her chances. He also helped Mary secure admission in Adimjati Government High School in Class 9.

Mary's school was a fair distance from SAI, and she woke up at 4 a.m. every day to cycle to the Academy. She would return at 8 a.m. and go to school. This was especially tough in Manipur's cold winter. She spent the next two years balancing her training and studies. When she felt that she was imposing on her relatives with her tight schedule, Mary rented an affordable house close to the training centre which she shared with a few friends. She cooked all her own meals. One of the girls who stayed with Mary was L. Sarita Devi. Sarita moved out after a while, but Mary stayed on as the rent was cheap.

At SAI, Mary tried out various sports like pole vault, javelin throw, and track and field events. Her coaches wanted her to try gymnastics, but Mary felt she was not suited to a sport which girls begin practicing at an early age. The truth was that none of these sports appealed to Mary, and she was keen on something that involved a little more action, like martial arts. Unfortunately, SAI Takyel focused only on track and field events and Mary decided to leave before the formal selections were done.

During this period, there was talk about women's boxing being introduced at SAI. This news excited Mary. Here was a sport that was right up her alley! After Dingko Singh of Manipur won the gold medal in the 1998 Bangkok Asian Games, there was a great buzz about boxing in the state. Dingko Singh was an iconic figure and Mary aspired to be a boxer like him. Along with

Dingko Singh, Mary Kom's other childhood icons were the legendary American boxer Muhammad Ali and his daughter Laila Ali.

THE LORD OF THE RING: DINGKO SINGH

Ngangom Dingko Singh was born into a poor family in Imphal's Sekta village. His parents were forced to leave him at a local orphanage and Dingko used his little fists to survive in a new hostile environment. Scouts from the Special Area Games Scheme (SAG) started by the Sports of Authority of India spotted his raw boxing talent.

He came into the limelight after winning the Sub-Junior National Boxing title at Ambala in 1989. He was ten years old at the time. His boxing career was launched and in 1997, Dingko won the King's Cup in Thailand, and was adjudged the Best Boxer of the meet.

Dingko famously threatened to commit suicide when the newspapers reported that he had been dropped from the 1998 Asiad squad.

Thankfully, Dingko was selected and proved his worth by clinching the gold medal in the 54 kg bantamweight category. This was an Asian Games boxing medal for India after sixteen years.

Dingko Singh received the Arjuna Award and the Padma Shri for his career-defining achievement. His victory began a sporting revolution in Manipur as boxers like Mary Kom and Laishram Sarita Devi decided to follow in his footsteps.

# *Chapter Four*

At a chance meeting with boxer Rebika Chiru, Mary learned that women's boxing had been introduced at SAI Khuman Lampak. She then learnt that the chief coach, L. Ibomcha Singh was one of the finest in the business and had produced several outstanding boxers over the years, besides being the national boxing champion in 1986. Mary decided to meet him. At the meeting, she told him straight away that she wanted to be coached by him. Ibomcha asked Mary to wait as he did not like to be disturbed while a training session was on. He met Mary after a long time, and asked her why she wanted to become a boxer.

'You are a small, frail girl who doesn't even look like a boxer,' he said. 'Boxing is for young boys.'

Mary looked so crestfallen that Ibomcha quickly asked about her parents and where she stayed.

'My training begins at six in the morning and lasts till nine. Then, it begins again at three in the afternoon till six in the evening,' Ibomcha declared after learning that Mary lived in Imphal now. 'You may join if you are interested and can keep up with this routine.'

Mary was overjoyed as she could now finally follow her dream! She began training a few days later. Ibomcha was a hard taskmaster but Mary was unaffected by the rigorous training. She soon realized that she was a born boxer with a natural flair and style.

*I have to train to perfect my footwork and punches* Mary thought, as she focused on specific boxing skills. There was no problem with her endurance levels. Mary was so obsessed with boxing that she ignored everything else. Everyone had to pitch in at the gym to keep it clean, along with the boxing hall and the yard. This was compulsory and meant to build cooperation and camaraderie among the trainees. But Mary didn't want to waste time doing anything else and received a good scolding from Ibomcha for this!

Right from her early boxing years, Mary adopted the strategy of being fast and furious in the ring. Intimidating an opponent early on was her strategy. She learnt everything she could from Ibomcha.

### THE FOUNDING FATHER OF MODERN MANIPURI BOXING

Boxing became a forgotten sport in Manipur after it faced an unofficial ban when trouble erupted during an exhibition match in the 1950s. The local crowd wanted to beat up a Bengali boxer who was adjudged the winner against the Manipuri boxer, leading to violent police action.

Thanks to L. Ibomcha Singh winning Manipur's first boxing medal, the sport regained its popularity in Manipur. A state champion between 1981 and 1986, and bronze medallist in the 1985 National Games, Ibomcha's boxing dreams were shattered just three hours before he was scheduled to fly to Thailand to make his international debut at the King's Cup. The Indian manager informed him that his name had been struck off the list. Ibomcha sadly bowed out of the boxing ring, vowing to pass on his knowledge. As coach, he churned out an impressive sixty-four international boxers, and was the founding father of women's boxing in India. As Mary Kom's coach, he has been immortalised in film and real life. 'No compromise, no excuse' was famously written on the wall of his training academy.

In 2010, the Indian government awarded Ibomcha Singh with the Dronacharya award for his invaluable services to Indian boxing.

In time, Mary became aware of the silent rivalry between the various boxing circles of Manipur. She heard rumours that SAI students might not be allowed to take part in state-level tournaments. So she decided to leave SAI in 2000 to qualify for the state-level tournament. Ibomcha did not object as he knew about this too. Mary shifted to the state coaching facility, but returned to Ibomcha right after the tournament.

After she left SAI, Mary trained for a few weeks with Oja Narjit of Youth Affairs and Sports (YAS) boxing academy. He was an enthusiastic coach who also served as guardian of the girls, arranging their accommodation in one of the buildings on the campus, and personally checking on their safety. Later, Mary shifted to Manipur Amateur Boxing Association (MABA), coaching under L. Kishan Singh. In just three months, Mary had trained under three good coaches, who enriched her boxing skills and insight into the sport. In her very first state championships,

Mary defeated Humbi in the finals, who had been one of her coaches when she began boxing at SAI.

Back home, Mary's parents had to work twice as hard because of her absence. Mary barely went home now, and did so only when she needed money or rice. She had kept her entry into boxing a secret from her parents, knowing her father wouldn't approve. Imphal was unknown territory for Mary's parents, who did not dare to venture there too often. But they sent Mary whatever they could—Rs 50 occasionally, and sometimes Rs 100 every month. Mary handled her own life in Imphal, and bought her first boxing gloves with Rs 350 saved from her pocket money. She trained without proper equipment as they were expensive, and couldn't even afford a pair of comfortable shoes that she badly needed. She managed with a cheap imitation of an original brand.

Mary was selected in the 48 kg category in the State Women's Boxing Championships, and went on to win the gold. She was also chosen as the Best Boxer of the Tournament. Although there was no prize money, Mary was overjoyed as it secured her a place in the state selections and gave her a chance to prove herself at the national level. But Mary was worried too. How would she let her family know? Thankfully, the local newspaper did the job on her behalf, reporting on the State Championships with her name misspelt as 'Maki Kom'.

Mary's father was travelling to Moirang on his bicycle one day, when he overheard some men reading the newspaper and talking.

'See! Now even women have started boxing in Manipur!'

Mary's father had a look at the grainy photograph in the newspaper, and couldn't recognize Mary. But he wasn't aware of any other Kom girl in SAI other than his daughter.

*This girl is named Maki not Chungneijang!* He told himself.

Mary's original name was Chungneijang, but as almost no one could pronounce this name perfectly at SAI, she had changed it to Mary. When Mary's cousin Chungthang visited the Academy one day, and asked for Chungneijang, he was told there was no one there by that name. When he discovered about the name change, he advised Mary to keep her original name as it was derived from her grandmother's name.

So, even today, Mary's official name is Mangte Chungneijang Mary Kom, although she is mostly known as M.C. Mary Kom or Mary Kom.

# *Chapter Five*

The newspaper article perplexed Mary's father, and he carried the newspaper to a person in his village who could read. When the article was read aloud to him, Mary's father was troubled, and asked her mother to fetch Mary home on the pretext of discussing something urgent.

'Why are you interested in boxing?' he asked Mary after she arrived. 'You didn't even tell me about it, and I had to learn it from the newspaper. I do not like this at all.' He ordered her sternly to stop boxing, but Mary refused.

'I love boxing and will not stop. Please understand, Apa,' she said, and tried to convince him. He put forth many arguments, how it was a dangerous sport, and how she could get injured and he could not afford her treatment.

'If you like martial arts, why don't you take up judo or karate?' he suggested.

But Mary was adamant. Amateur boxing was not as dangerous as he thought, she explained. She explained the rules of amateur boxing and described all the protective gear that had to be used.

'Boxing is my dream sport,' Mary said passionately.

Eventually, her father calmed down and told her she could pursue boxing seriously.

Mary was relieved that her parents now

supported her decision. They worked even harder, her mother weaving at night to save all the money she could to send to her daughter. All her parents' resources were directed towards the fulfillment of Mary's dream to box for India. Mary's other dream was to secure a government job through the sports quota. 'I will buy a Pulsar bike with my first prize money,' she said to her mother. 'I'll buy a farm for Apa and a car for you.'

Mother and daughter laughed together at these silly dreams, but, deep down in her heart, Mary was determined to give her parents a better life.

The first time Mary stepped outside Manipur was to participate in the Seventh East India Open Boxing Championships in Kolkata, in 2000. In a surprising gesture, representatives of the Kom-Rem Student Union came to see Mary off at the

bus station, presenting her with Rs 500 and a traditional sarong called the phanek.

'Wear this on the victory stand!' they said. That was the moment when Mary knew that she had to win for herself as well as for her people.

Mary had lived her entire life in a small village in Manipur, and a little of it in the capital, Imphal. She had no idea of the outside world. As soon as she reached Guwahati, the capital of Assam, and ventured further beyond the north-east, she realized that she had never seen so many people gathered in one place ever. The pace and colour of this new world and the immense possibilities in it thrilled Mary.

Mary won gold in the tournament, sealing a berth in the Manipur state team. The next year, Mary Kom participated in her first major tournament—the First National Women's Boxing Championships held in Chennai in 2001. She was chosen in the 48 kg category, and travelled by train for the first time in her life. She won gold here as well. The Manipur women's boxing team and coach Oja Kishan travelled to Bangalore from there to attend a training camp. There, Mary was introduced to a retinue of different exercises, including speed training and gym workouts.

That same year, Mary had to travel to Hisar for training and selection to the first Asian Women's Boxing Championship. She travelled alone, and her suitcase got robbed when the train passed through Bihar at night. All her money and belongings, including her passport were gone! Mary burst into loud sobs as all hopes of participating in the international tournament seemed to sink. There was no way another passport could be made at such short notice. In Hisar, her colleagues and coach comforted her, and her father told her not to worry after learning what had happened. He sold the family cow to raise money for a new passport.

Mary was selected for the championship, but was helpless without a passport. Mary's father approached her uncle Songboi who entrusted a man to collect money from the Kom community in the Greater Imphal area. Then he called up his acquaintance in the passport office.

'A new passport in a day?' the man exclaimed. 'You're asking for a miracle.'

But when the situation was explained to him, he performed that miracle. Songboi's brother flew to Guwahati with the required documents, and another Kom who was the superintendent of police, Imphal East, helped speed up the paperwork. The passport was dispatched to Delhi when it was ready. It was collected by Karung Onkholer, a Manipuri footballer popularly known as Onler Kom, who arrived with it to Hisar, six hours away, to deliver it to Mary. The Koms had saved the day again, and it was the beginning of a beautiful friendship between Mary and Onler Kom.

Mary Kom is married to the footballer Karung Onkholer (Onler). She first met Onler in 2000 when he was studying law at Delhi University.

Onler was the president of the North East student's body then and helped Mary get her new passport. They became friends, and soon started dating and got married in 2005.

As Mary herself admits, Onler left a full-fledged football career to take care of their children so that she could pursue her boxing dreams.

'After my marriage, my husband has been a pillar of my strength,' Mary Kom shared with Indian cricket superstar Virat Kohli on an Instagram chat. 'The support he gives me is immense. He takes care of everything that I can ask for; he is the ideal husband and father.'

# Chapter Six

Mary travelled out of India for the first time when she went to Bangkok. But all the stress and the worry to get there took its toll and she was defeated in her first match to an opponent who was bigger and stronger, and who also had the partisan support of the home crowd. It was a big lesson for her, and she vowed to fight always with her body as well as her mind. Mary promised to make a better impression in the World Championships in the USA, only a few months away.

The USA was an expensive place, and Mary had to carry some money with her. Her father could rustle up only Rs 2000 for the trip. A worried Mary spoke to Onler about the situation, who organized a meeting with a few students and elders from the Kom community to solve this problem. They discussed how they could raise money for Mary's trip.

The president of the Kom-Rem Union, Manipur, Pu. Lalkhomang was in Delhi then and was present at this meeting. He asked the students to meet the two Manipuri Members of Parliament and seek their help. This was a good suggestion as the two MPs, Holkhomang Haokip and Choaba Singh donated Rs 5000 and Rs 3000 respectively. Now, Mary had the princely sum of Rs 10,000 with her and some more money that the Manipuri community had collected for her.

Mary was relieved to be going to the US with some money in hand. She could not forget the kindness and love of her community members. *I cannot return empty-handed from the USA* Mary thought. So she promised herself that she would win a medal at the event.

When Mary reached Pennsylvania in the USA, she was exhausted because of jet-lag, and was relieved to know that she didn't have a match that day, unlike some of her other team members. She got some rest before her first round, which she won comfortably. As her team members lost one by one, Mary reached the finals of the 48 kg category, but lost to Hula Sahin of Turkey 13–5.

When Mary analysed her failure, she figured

it could be because of her loss of appetite as she could not eat the food that was offered in the US, and had lost weight. Mary was so disappointed to lose the gold that she cried in her room. The coaches consoled Mary as she was the only one on the team who had won a medal. But Mary's biggest takeaway from this championship was that she could face any boxer in the world.

Everything in the US was so expensive that all Mary could buy was a few candies for her family. Back home in India, the media was not interested that an Indian boxer had won the silver medal in the first edition of a world championship event as women's boxing was at a nascent stage. But Mary was welcomed with garlands, drumbeats and dancing in Imphal. This was followed by a victory march, felicitations, and a grand feast. It was the first sporting achievement by anyone from the Kom tribe, and that too an international achievement. The medal came with an announcement by the Sports Ministry of an award of Rs 9 lakh. When Mary finally got the money almost a year later, the first thing she did with it was to buy a paddy field for her father. She was determined that he would no longer be a landless farmer. Then, she set aside money for the education of her brother and sister, as she wanted them to have what she couldn't.

Mary also donated a small sum to MABA as she felt her coaches were instrumental for her success. She bought a two-wheeler for herself, and set aside some money for her training and travels in her quest for gold. A silver medal simply wasn't enough.

Onler's support for Mary's boxing career only deepened their friendship. As he was a sportsman himself, Mary always sought his advice and he became her emotional anchor. Mary only had a little free time on Sundays after a grueling week of training sessions and tours. That was when she'd meet up with Onler and spend time with him. He was her only friend outside the boxing circles.

Mary Kom's workout plan combined strength training, cardio, and boxing drills. She trained for six days a week and took one day off for rest and recovery.

- Strength Training: Mary focused on building strength in her upper body, lower body and core muscles with exercises like push-ups, pull-ups, squats, lunges, and planks to strengthen her muscles.

- Cardio: Cardio exercises like running, skipping, and cycling to boost her endurance and stamina.
- Boxing Drills: Shadowboxing, heavy bag work, speed bag work and sparring to improve her technique and footwork.

Mary Kom's diet plan included proteins like eggs, chicken, fish and lentils, carbohydrates like brown rice, whole wheat bread, and sweet potatoes, and fruits and vegetables for essential vitamins and minerals.

In 2003, Mary received the Arjuna Award, which was a huge boost to her career. Now her parents started to receive numerous marriage proposals for her. Although marriage was not on Mary's agenda, Onler was worried she would give up boxing after her marriage—a common trend among women sportspersons in India. Besides, Onler did not want to lose Mary, and he proposed to her. Mary was confused as she was fond of Onler, but not ready for marriage. On the other hand, Onler would be the perfect partner for her as he had always been so supportive of her boxing career.

'I will never come between you and your career,' Onler promised Mary, and she agreed to marry him. Onler called up his father to share the news with him, and discovered that Onler's mother was closely related to Mary's grandfather. The two realized that common roots and fate had brought them together.

Mary's father was dead against her marriage

as he wanted her to focus only on her boxing career. The traditional manner in which a boy's family asked for a girl's hand in marriage was by boiling tea in the girl's house. This ritual is done thrice before the wedding date is finalized. The first tea-boiling session is normally a hush-hush ceremony, attended by few people. Onler's father arrived to be welcomed warmly by Mary's maternal uncle. But the second time Onler's parents arrived at Mary's house with a few family members, Mary's father did not allow them inside the house. This act embarrassed and angered Mary so much that she left home to stay in a friend's place. Mary even told Onler that they should elope and get married. Onler refused to marry Mary without obtaining her father's permission.

‘Let us not disgrace our families,’ he said to Mary. Slowly, Mary’s father cooled down as he realized that Onler was an honourable man. He sent a messenger to Onler’s family, inviting them to come and boil tea at his house. A date was fixed for the wedding, and Mary and Onler got married on 12 March 2005. It was one of the most beautiful days of Mary’s life as she exchanged rings and vows with the man she loved. The feast, festivity, singing and dancing continued throughout the night.

# Chapter Seven

After her marriage, Mary took a four-month break from boxing to settle into her new life. Her family elders had instructed Mary that she would have to wake up early, do the household chores, and cook for her in-laws. But in her new village and home, her in-laws were very cooperative and wanted Mary to focus on boxing.

A month later, the couple returned to Imphal where Mary had been allotted a house at the National Games Village by the Government of Manipur. The Village had been converted into government quarters after the 1999 National Games. Mary started training for the Asian Boxing Championships and World Championships, and Onler managed the house as Mary travelled from camp to camp. The couple kept in touch everyday thanks to their mobile phones.

Mary realized that she needed to look for a job for a steady income. She had a lot of dependents and even travelling for work required money. Besides, the career of a sportswoman was a short one. But all that she managed to get was the job of a police constable, which she declined as not befitting a player who had won a World Championship silver and gold medal for India. Thankfully, in 2005, the Manipur government offered Mary the post of a sub-inspector after she won her second World Championship gold. Her dream of getting a government job through the sports quota was finally fulfilled. This job did not entail Mary to go for work regularly, and she could focus on her boxing totally.

Mary's medal haul continued after her marriage, putting an end to speculation from all corners, including her family, that her career would end post marriage. From 2001 to 2004, Mary Kom had a golden run, bagging the first position in all the Senior Women's National Championships, the second World Women's Boxing Championship, the second Asian Women's Boxing Championship, and the Witch Cup Boxing Championships at Hungary. In 2005, Mary retained her title in the third World Women's Boxing Championships in Russia.

L. Sarita won the bronze, and both women were given a hero's welcome at Imphal airport by a huge crowd. In 2005, Mary was selected for the prestigious Padma Shri, India's fourth-highest civilian award .

Mary also won international championships in Taiwan, Vietnam and Denmark. But one of her superlative achievements was retaining her world title in 2006 by beating a powerful opponent in Steluta Duta of Romania 22–7. This win in Delhi was particularly memorable for Mary as all her family members and relatives had come to watch the bout. Thanks to this hat-trick of World Championship victories, the media named Mary Kom 'the Queen of Boxing' and 'Magnificent Mary'.

But Mary's perfect world collapsed one day because of a terrible incident. Since the 1980s, Manipur had seen insurgency with over thirty militant groups, each running parallel governments with their own constitutions, especially in remote villages without police or army security. Some of these insurgents kidnapped Mary's father-in-law, and he was discovered dead. Onler was devastated. Mary was so dejected that she considered giving up boxing.

Insurgency in Manipur can be traced back to 1964 with the formation of the United National Liberation Front (UNLF), one of the most intimidating militant outfits.

This separatist insurgency rose from the discontent over the alleged forced merger of Manipur with the Union of India and the delay in granting Manipur full-fledged statehood. The kingdom of Manipur was merged with India on 15 October 1949, but became a state only in 1972.

Later years saw the rise of several militant outfits demanding an independent Manipur like the People's Liberation Army (PLA), People's Revolutionary Party of Kangleipak (PREPAK), Kangleipak Communist Party (KCP), and Kanglei Yawol Kanna Lup (KYKL), among others.

Currently, ethnic violence in Manipur has erupted into a kind of civil war because of tensions between two groups, the majority Meitei tribe and the minority Kuki tribe, who are battling each other over land and power.

Back in Imphal, Onler's thoughts were centred on revenge. He wanted to hunt down the killers of his father, even if that meant joining the insurgency. Some friends offered to get him a .32 revolver so he could hunt down the killers with the same weapon they had used to kill his father. Mary tried to pacify him but failed. A tormented Onler was so consumed by thoughts of revenge that he was almost losing his sanity. Then, when their family threatened to fall apart, a miracle happened to change everything.

Mary discovered she was pregnant. A big change came over Onler when he learnt the news and his bitterness disappeared. His joy knew no bounds when the ultrasound later revealed that Mary would have twins. Onler's father, too, had been one in a pair of twins. Onler felt like his father was being reborn.

On 5 August 2007, Mary became the proud mother of two beautiful, identical baby boys. Motherhood was another feather in her illustrious cap. After the twins were born in 2007, Mary Kom was blessed with another son in 2013. In 2018, Mary and Onler decided to expand their family further and adopted a girl named Merilyn.

# *Chapter Eight*

Life changed drastically for Mary after becoming a mother. Onler and Mary spent many sleepless nights as the twins kept them awake. Soon, the time to name the twins arrived. This was a serious affair in the Kom community where the opinions of all the elders in the family are sought. After a long session, Mary's father came up with the idea of naming them 'Worldthang' or 'Worldchung', adding 'world' to their names in honour of Mary's World Championship titles. It was common for the village children to be named after a significant event or prized possession of the family. A child was once named 'Cyclethang' after his father had bought a cycle.

Mary remained with her children for one and a half years. Thankfully, no major international tournaments were held during Mary's two-year sabbatical from boxing. Mary recovered quickly, and began exercising to build up her stamina. The doctor had advised rest for three years but Mary

was ready for a comeback. She wanted to prove all the doubters wrong, including her own family.

Mary really missed her father-in-law as he was the one who would encourage her the most in her boxing career. When her own parents advised her to quit boxing as they felt she had achieved a lot, her father-in-law was always supportive. 'Let her play as long as she wants,' he would say to Onler. But now, he was not around to help her in this difficult phase.

When Mary left for the training camp for selections to the fourth Asian Women's Championships, her twins were a little over a year old. The decision to part from her twins had been a particularly tough one for Mary. But the thought that she would never box again spurred her on to take this difficult decision.

After a few weeks of training, Mary was sick and in terrible pain. The painkiller prescribed helped, and Mary was determined to continue training. Somehow, Mary got through the camp with the nausea, aches and pains, fighting the urge to hang up her boxing gloves. The looks of her teammates suggested that Mary's career was over, but her dogged determination saw Mary being selected for the tournament in Guwahati in September 2008. Mary reached the semi-final to beat Nguyen Thi Hoa of Vietnam and entered the final to face Jong Ok of North Korea. Mary had defeated her earlier, but Jong Ok had the last laugh this time, and Mary had to settle for silver.

For someone making a comeback after two years, this was a tremendous achievement. But Mary wasn't satisfied and promised to do better next time. Mary realized that she had to work on her fitness as the techniques used in training patterns in India were outdated. She did not even have a dietician to monitor her food and gauge her fitness. Thankfully, by now Mary had a sponsor, and a specialist doctor was assigned to her. She was advised to increase her calcium intake, and thanks to the personal attention towards nutrition, physical health, and improved training, Mary bounced back into shape quickly. She worked harder than before to clinch gold at the ninth Senior Women's Championship, and this was a great morale booster before the upcoming fifth World Championship in Ningbo, China.

Mary loved Ningbo which was full of shopping malls. For the first time, she had enough money to shop for everyone in her family. Mary reached the final where she would face her old rival, Steluta Duta of Romania. Mary decided not to take her opponent lightly and focused on practice and training, declining the invitations to guided tours. The sacrifice paid off as Mary demolished the Romanian 7-1 in a one-sided final. Magnificent Mary was back with a historic fourth gold to become the most successful woman boxer in the world! This win was significant as women's boxing had picked up, and the competition had intensified.

In 2009, Mary received the prestigious Rajiv Gandhi Khel Ratna Award with a prize money of Rs 7.5 lakh. But she faced the biggest challenge of her boxing career when she received the news of her younger son Rengpa's illness just before the 2011 Asian Cup in Haikou, China. Out of maternal instinct, Mary suggested to Onler over the telephone to take along their other son Nainai to the pediatrician as well. The doctor prescribed medicines for Rengpa's cold and fever, but after examining Nainai, he discovered an irregular heartbeat. Further investigations revealed that he had a hole in his heart. Mary and Onler were stunned as the three-year-old had never shown any symptoms of sickness. They decided to take Nainai to Chandigarh for treatment as they had friends there. The doctor there advised them to admit Nainai for surgery just a few days before the Asian Cup.

Mary wanted to skip the competition, but her family and Onler insisted that she go. Mary left for China with a heavy heart, and spoke to

Onler every day to learn that Nainai was fine and the operation would happen after she returned. Mary knew she had to make the effort of staying away from her family during this crucial hour count, and she did so by winning the gold. While the Indian contingent celebrated, Mary was desperate to get to Chandigarh.

The team reached Delhi at night, and Mary's sponsors IOS arranged for her speedy travel to Chandigarh. Mary reached just in time to see her son being wheeled into the operation theatre. After assuring him that she was there now, she let go of his hand and prayed to God. The surgery went on for several hours, and Nainai was finally wheeled out with several tubes attached to his body. He was in the ICU for three days, with Mary keeping constant vigil beside him. Nainai was discharged after a long stay, hale and hearty but for a scar which the family named the Spiderman scar.

Even though Mary had to travel frequently for her boxing commitments, she was happiest when she stayed home with her children. She remains a strong advocate of children's rights, firmly believing that children are the hope for the future and the source of all happiness.

> Mary Kom is also an animal rights activist. As a Member of Parliament in the Rajya Sabha, she has strongly advocated animal rights activism.
>
> She supports PETA, the world's leading animal rights activist group. One of the biggest campaigns Mary Kom was involved in was to end the use of elephants in circus performances in India. She is also responsible for including PETA's humane education programme in school syllabus.

# *Chapter Nine*

Mary travelled to Bridgetown, Barbados to participate for the sixth time in the World Boxing Championships. Mary had won silver in the inaugural edition and four golds after that. Mary's previous weight category, 46 kg, was redundant now, and she was participating in the 48 kg category. Mary reached the finals to be pitted again against her old rival Steluta Duta.

In the first round, Steluta had the upper hand, leading 4-3. But Mary made a strong comeback in the second round, and won the match after

the third round 16-6. Mary Kom had won a record fifth gold medal at the World Boxing Championships !

Thousands of people thronged the airport complex when Mary returned to Imphal, and she was taken in an open jeep through the city so the crowds could see their champion. The chief minister, O. Ibobi Singh was the chief guest in

Mary's welcome ceremony, and he gave Mary an incentive award of Rs 10 lakh, and announced her promotion to Additional Superintendent of Police. Now, Mary had her eyes set on the Olympics, as after so many years of boxing she had finally got the chance to participate in the prestigious event in the 2012 Games in London. She was the only female boxer from India to qualify for the London Olympics.

The road to the Olympics had not been an easy one and Mary had to fight her way to seal that berth. The first challenge Mary faced was that her weight category was not included in the Olympics, and she had to increase her weight up to 51 kg to compete. This also meant facing bigger and taller opponents in the ring. The ideal opportunity to test her skills before the

Olympics arrived with the 2010 Asian Games in Guangzhou, China, where women's boxing had been included for the first time in three weight categories—51 kg, 60 kg, and 75 kg.

The trials to select the team that would go to China were held. L. Sarita, Meena Kumari, and Pinky Jangra were also competing for the berth in the 51 kg category.

Mary had to compete against boxers from five weight categories to qualify for the 51 kg fly-weight category. Mary beat Sarita to qualify for the Asian Games. However, she lost to China's Ren Cancan 11-7 in the semi-final at the Asian Games and returned with a bronze medal. The defeat was not surprising as it was an unfamiliar weight category but Mary was very disappointed as she was aiming for gold as usual. She worked harder than ever to prepare for the Olympics. The next time Mary met Cancan at the sixth Asian Boxing Championships in 2012, she emerged as the winner.

Since 2011, Mary had been training with a foreign coach as she had realized that was the only way to compete on the international stage. Under British coach Charles Atkinson, Mary made rapid strides. Atkinson had proved his coaching mettle earlier by taking Thai male boxing to another level in the 1980s. The only problem was that he did not have an AIBA three-star certificate, a must for an official Olympic coach.

Atkinson's lessons improved Mary's fighting style considerably as the focus was on punches, strength, guard, and various combinations. Earlier, someone had said that when Mary boxes, she hits her opponents bop-bop-bop. But thanks to Atkinson, Mary's defence became strong, and her counterattack improved using a combination of punches and jabs. Mary also learnt how to change her defensive moves according to her opponent's boxing style.

Mary's sponsors Olympic Gold Quest (OGQ) ensured she had access to top-class infrastructure and also took care of her travel and stay. Physiotherapist Janhavi Jathar monitored Mary's health and recovery from childbirth, and also stayed in Imphal with Mary for a while to supervise her initial exercises. The doctor's assistance was invaluable for Mary as she needed to increase her weight scientifically through proper nutritional intake. It took her six months to gain one and a half kilos. The opposite was true for the two top contenders in the Olympics, Ren Cancan and Nicola Adams, who were fighting in the 54 kg category earlier and were now struggling to reduce weight. Both boxers were taller and stronger than Mary. Mary also had to be careful to keep the fat off as that would slow her down in the ring.

Winning the gold at the sixth Asian Women's Boxing Championships at Mongolia was a great morale booster for Mary. She was now raring to go for the World Championships in Qinhuang-dao, China, where boxers would eventually qualify for the Olympics. It was the only qualifying event for the historic debut of women's boxing at the Olympics.

Mary received a bye in the first round, and beat the Japanese boxer Ayako Minowa 20-9 in the next round. Mary beat Narielle Hanson of Norway in the next round 26-16 to progress to the quarter-finals, where she faced Nicola Adams. Mary planned her strategy by watching videos of Nicola's fights. It was an intense and close bout, which Mary lost 13-11. Although devastated, Mary watched the semi-final between Adams and the Russian Elena Savelyeva with baited breath as her Olympic ticket depended on that bout. Elena had defeated the North Korean Hye Kim, and Adams had beat Mary. The rule stated that if Adams won, Mary would go through, and if Elena won, Hye Kim would progress. Mary had never rooted for any opponent the way she cheered Nicola Adams that day, who won 11-6.

Mary was elated. She had become the first Indian woman boxer to qualify for the Olympics.

Mary even forgot the disappointment of her loss in her euphoria in qualifying for the London Olympics.

> The history of women's boxing can be traced to 1720 though it existed as a sport residing in the shadow of other sports for a long time.
>
> In 1876, the first female boxing match within the United States was held at the New York Hills theatre as Nell Saunders and Rose Harland faced each other in the ring. This fight became a part of women's culture and history later, but also had the strangest prize for the winner—a silver butter dish!
>
> In the 1904 Olympic Games, women's boxing first made its appearance as a demonstration and exhibition sport. Only the USA competed with eighteen boxers.

The Olympic committee decided that boxing was a health risk for women, and restricted the sport to men. Boxing became the only sport that did not include women.

The 2012 London Olympics was a landmark event as not only was women's boxing included for the first time, but this was the first Olympic Games where every sport had female competitors.

# Chapter Ten

Mary's sponsors OGQ had organized a month-long training camp at the Balewadi Sports Complex in Pune. Mary obtained permission from the Sports Ministry to train there separately. This was convenient because at the national training camp, one coach was assigned to more than twenty women simultaneously, while Mary could train at Balewadi with handpicked sparring partners.

Mary enjoyed this training which commenced from March 2012. MABA sent local training partners from Manipur so that Mary could communicate with them easily. Coach Oja Kishan arrived with the three boxers Onler and Mary had selected in Manipur based on their height and boxing style. They resembled Mary's probable opponents in the Olympics in height and weight and were disciplined boxers who wouldn't cause Mary any injury before the Games.

Four camps were conducted in total, and for the last one, Charles Atkinson and Mary selected junior boys from the Army Sports Institute in Pune as Mary's sparring partners. Before the Olympics, two weeks of training sessions were also held in Liverpool, Atkinson's home turf.

In July 2012, Mary boarded the flight to London, leaving early to acclimatise to English conditions. Her dream moment had finally arrived! On reaching Heathrow, Mary felt like a small matador facing a huge, angry bull. There were posters everywhere advertising the Games, and Mary's stomach fluttered with anticipation. She was relieved to see her coach's familiar face when she reached Liverpool. Charles had become like a father figure for Mary, and he arranged a boxing gym and sparring partners for Mary to practice. Mary considered herself lucky to be training under Charles, and regretted his absence when she had to move in with the rest of the Indian contingent to the Olympic Games Village a few days before the women's boxing events began.

The women's boxing bouts were scheduled towards the end of the Games. Mary relaxed and tried to conserve her energy, practicing in the morning and evening by herself. Anoop Kumar, the chief coach of the women's boxing team helped Mary. As she had joined the Indian team quite late at the Village, Mary could barely meet the others who were busy with their practice and events. She met other Indian athletes in the dining hall, and they greeted each other. Mary already knew Gagan Narang and Vijay Kumar as they were also sponsored by OGQ. She sought out the talented young Manipuri boxer, Devendro Singh to speak to him. After Devendro lost, Mary consoled him, and asked him not to be disheartened as he had a long career ahead of him.

Mary had to keep checking her weight and eat whenever it went down to keep up with the required weight in her category. But the food was too sweet for her, and Mary indulged in a heavy breakfast as the menu was more to her liking than the lunch or dinner served there.

Mary's mother and Onler arrived in London before her first Olympic bout, and Mary went to meet them at their hotel, which was far from the Village. Her family's presence really lifted Mary's spirits, and she was geared up for her match the next day.

'Please pray for me, Apa,' Mary told her father on the phone before her first bout.

'I'm always praying for you,' he replied. 'Don't worry! I am confident you won't return empty-handed from the Olympics. May God bless you!'

Mary faced Karolina Michalczuk of Poland on August 5. It was a special day for Mary as her twins had been born on this day. She managed to calm her nervousness, and faced her opponent. But Karolina was so strong that Mary felt she was hitting a concrete wall when her punches landed. Mary lost her footing to fall during the match. But she realized that her opponent lacked technique and used her counter-attacking skills, unleashing powerful hooks directed at her opponent's head to win the bout decisively: 19-4.

The support of the fans overwhelmed Mary during her match as they cheered her on and shouted her name repeatedly. She saw the familiar faces of Bijoy Koi-jam Sir and Dileep Sir, who had travelled all the way from Manipur to support her. Mary was indebted to the European Manipuri Association (EMA) for their support. Later, Mary dedicated the victory to her sons in front of the Indian media. The first hurdle had been crossed successfully.

The second bout was the next day, and Mary faced Maroua Rahali of Tunisia. Mary went defensive in the first two rounds, but still won them. In the third round, Mary launched a fierce attack, returning to her bop-bop-bop style to surprise Rahali with the sudden change of pace. Mary won the bout 15-6. She was in the semi-finals now, and assured of an Olympic medal. Mary had her eyes firmly set on the gold medal.

After just one day's rest, Mary faced Nicola Adams on 8 August. Adams had the advantage of height and reach, and although Mary did most of the attacking in the bout, she could not get close enough to hit Adams. The first bout against Karolina had also taken a toll on Mary. Her body was stiff, and her movements and feet were slower than usual. Adams won 11-6, and went on to win the Olympic gold in the final. Mary was dejected after the loss, but she had given it her very best. As she left the hall, Mary received a standing ovation from the spectators. But her Olympic run had ended!

The 2012 London Olympic Games saw India enter the fray with eighty-three competitors. It was India's most successful outing ever until Tokyo 2020.

In London, India won 6 Olympic medals, including 2 silver and 4 bronze. India bettered this in Tokyo 2020 with 7 medals, including 1 gold, 2 silver, and 4 bronze.

# *Chapter Eleven*

As soon as Mary stepped out of the stadium, she was surrounded by journalists, who fired non-stop questions at her. A disheartened Mary did not want to talk to any of them. Later, during a live video conference on television with Indian sports stars Prakash Padukone and Geet Sethi, she said sorrowfully to them as well as to all Indians, 'I am sorry I could not win gold.'

Mary's father consoled her with wise words when she called him on the phone and broke down. 'The gold is not your birthright,' he said.

'God gave you what you deserve. I am very happy you got an Olympic medal. There will be other moments. Now, be thankful for what you have received.'

Charles was of the same opinion, and he told the media later that Mary was the better fighter in the bout and Adams won only because of her defensive tactics. Mary was a little relieved, but still had a feeling that she had let down her country by not winning the gold medal. Little did she realize the enormity of what she had achieved as an Olympic medal was every athlete's dream.

> India has won three Olympic medals in boxing and all the medals have been bronze.
>
> Haryana-born Vijender Singh was the first boxer to begin the trend at the Beijing 2008

Olympics when he won the bronze in the Men's 75 kg category to become the poster boy of Indian boxing.

Mary Kom from Manipur repeated the feat in the 2012 London Olympics, winning the bronze medal in the Women's 51 kg category, and cementing her place as the greatest Indian boxer of all time.

Assamese Lovlina Borgohain made her Olympic debut at Tokyo 2020. She beat experienced opponents to clinch the bronze and take Mary Kom's legacy forward.

It was time to say goodbye to London, and Mary's plane landed in New Delhi airport in the early hours of the morning. After Mary stepped into the arrivals lounge, she was surprised when she was suddenly surrounded by guards, who ushered her away without telling her where they were taking her.

*Where are Onler and Mother?* Mary thought in panic. But the guards wouldn't answer her questions. After Mary stepped outside, she understood and comprehended the strange behaviour of the guards. Even though the day had just begun, the airport was crowded with people. Bands were playing music and everyone tried to garland Mary at once, resulting in a huge commotion. Mary had never received such a rousing, emotional and overwhelming welcome in her entire life. That's when the enormity of her achievement struck her.

To avoid the huge crowd, Mary was swiftly guided to a vehicle. The vehicle began going forward, but had only managed to move a few inches when it was stopped by the media, who wanted to interview Mary. After the car had moved a hundred metres, Mary had had enough. She wanted to meet her family and see her children who had come to the airport to receive her. She threatened to jump off the vehicle if it didn't return to the airport. Immediately, her request was met. As Mary reached the airport

again, she met some Kom students who helped her find her family. It was a joyous reunion with her sons as they hugged each other.

Seizing their chance, the Kom students who had helped Mary locate her family, welcomed her with drums, gongs and the traditional dance. Mary happily joined in, finally celebrating her medal win.

After four days in Delhi, Mary left for Imphal. When they landed, they were greeted by a massive crowd at the airport. The sound of cheers and drums filled the air. Mary was welcomed in the arrivals lounge with a traditional sarong and shawl. A flower-decked open jeep took her and Devendro for a victory ride across Imphal town. It was raining but that did nothing to dampen the spirit of the crowds that had gathered on both sides of the street and greeted their champion with shouts of 'Long live Mary Kom'.

Flowers and garlands were thrown lovingly towards the vehicle that took the boxers to a reception at Khuman Lampak Sports Complex. The chief minister and other ministers of Manipur were present, along with the entire boxing community and the three other state Olympians—Laishram Bombayla Devi, Ng Soniya Chanu and Devendro Singh.

Mary received a cheque of Rs 75 lakh from the chief minister. The government announced her promotion to the rank of Superintendent of Police (Sports) and also allotted her three acres of land to run the M.C. Mary Kom Boxing Academy, which was her dream project to train youngsters in the sport she had perfected.

# *Chapter Twelve*

Mary had first got the idea for a boxing academy in 2005 when she visited Mokokching village in Manipur to attend a function. There, she met the younger sister of her sister-in-law, Nengneihat, and saw that she had the potential to be a good boxer. Mary was impressed with Nengneihat's build, height, and strong boyish appearance. She was an orphan who was staying with her relatives. Mary asked her elders for permission, and took the girl under her wing. She brought Nengneihat home with her, and began teaching her the basics of boxing. The girl was a quick learner, and soon became Mary's regular sparring partner when she practiced at home.

Slowly, the news that Mary Kom was teaching a student spread like wildfire, and several parents approached Mary with the request that she teach boxing to their kids. Mary could not say no to all of them, and began training a few of them. The number of students training under Mary increased steadily, and Onler suggested to his wife that she open a boxing academy. That is how the idea of the M.C. Mary Kom Boxing Academy was born with the noble intention of teaching the students absolutely free of charge with a special focus on underprivileged children. Boxing had given so much to Mary that she wanted to give something back to her community. What better way than passing on her skills so that boxing developed further in her home state?

Mary established her academy in her own backyard in 2006. At the time, she did not have access to proper infrastructure, and there was also no boxing ring. All Mary had was her talent and experience and Onler's support. With the government finally coming to their aid, the future certainly looked promising. Mary began scouting for players from poor families who might have hidden potential for boxing. Most of her students were in their teens, but some were as young as ten. Mary bore all the expenses, including the food and lodging of these students, and the salaries of an extra coach and the warden of the hostel. Most months, her entire pay went behind the academy. But it was the best investment Mary had made as Nengneihat won gold at the All-India Inter-Sai in 2008, followed by silver the following year. She also won two golds at the state level, and silver and bronze at the national level.

Mary Kom's academy was taken seriously only after her students began winning medals. T.S. Merina Chiru won gold at the second National Women's Sub-Junior Boxing Championships in 2011. K. Oneithang Kom won gold at the state level, followed by silver. OGQ sponsored Nengneihat and Oneithang, as medal potentials for India, which was a great achievement for the academy. 2010 saw Mary's academy upgraded to a regional academy and renamed M.C. Mary Kom Regional Boxing Foundation. Now, the academy caters to the entire north-east of India.

Issues like infrastructure and accommodation improved with the active support of the Indian army, which has a great boxing culture. The army donated boxing gear, a generator, a gymnasium and also kitchen equipment to Mary's academy. Since 2010, SAI Manipur has been providing sports kits for Mary's students as well as a stipend of Rs 600 per student.

Mary Kom is the epitome of women's empowerment. Her life story is a fantastic source of inspiration for not just women athletes or women boxers, but for anyone who faces constant challenges in the pursuit of their dreams. Despite the handicaps in her background, she managed to break all the barriers and overcome all hurdles to reach the pinnacle of a difficult sport and also made a mark in the lives of so many others .

Mary Kom finally hung up her boxing gloves aged forty-one, thus drawing the curtain on a long and remarkable boxing career. What made Mary stop eventually was the International Boxing Association rules that allow male and female boxers to fight in elite-level competitions only till the age of forty.

'I have the hunger still but unfortunately because of the age limit it is over. I cannot compete in any competition. I want to play more but I am being forced to quit (due to the age limit). I have to retire. I have achieved everything in my life,' Mary Kom said famously.

In 2012, Mary Kom handed over the keys of a Bolero to her father as a Christmas gift, thus keeping the promise she had once jokingly made to her mother. Despite Mary's repeated requests, her parents refused to shift to town to live with her, preferring to stay in Kangathei with their relatives and friends. They haven't changed much although their house has—it has been transformed with new rooms added, along with a cooking gas in the kitchen. The granary is filled with rice to last a year, and a tractor has replaced the bullocks on the field.

'I believe with all my heart that if you pursue

your dream with all the zeal at your command, nothing is impossible. I dared to dream big in spite of my humble beginnings. I hope that my life is proof to youngsters across India that it is possible to do more if they dare, if they have the will.'—Mary Kom

SOME AMAZING BOXING FACTS

- The precise origins of boxing are unknown to us. But the earliest form of boxing can be traced to 6000 BCE in Ethiopia in Africa. From there, it spread to Egypt around 3000 BCE and then to ancient Mesopotamia, ancient Greece, and Rome.
- In 1949, a boxing match took place between a man named Gus Waldorf and an unnamed

bear. The bear won, despite the handicap of having its mouth muzzled, claws filed, and boxing gloves fitted.

- Once, Mike Tyson nearly fought against a gorilla in the 1980s. He saw a large silverback gorilla in the zoo bullying the weaker gorillas and offered the zookeeper $10,000 to open the enclosure so he could teach the gorilla a lesson. Luckily for the gorilla, the zookeeper refused Iron Mike's offer.
- Hollywood star Liam Neeson was a former amateur boxing champion. He started boxing as a nine year old at his local club in Northern Ireland and continued till he was seventeen.
- The longest bout in boxing history took place on 6 April 1893 in New Orleans, Louisiana, USA, between Jack Burke and Andy Bowen. It lasted for 110 rounds— 7 hours and 19 minutes!

# *Mary Kom:* *A Timeline*

- 1982: Mangte Chungneijang Mary Kom is born in Kangathei village, Manipur, to Mangte Tonpa Kom and Mangte Akham Kom.
- 1998: Mary Kom decides to take up boxing inspired by Dingko Singh's gold medal at the Asian Games.
- 2000: Wins silver at AIBA (International Boxing Association) Women's World Championships.

- 2002: Wins gold at AIBA Women's World Championships.
- 2003: Wins gold at Asian Women's Championships and recipient of the Arjuna Award.
- 2005: Marries K. Onler Kom.
- 2006: Recipient of the Padma Shri Award.
- 2007: Takes a break from boxing to be with her newly born twins.
- 2008: Makes her comeback in boxing to win gold at AIBA Women's World Championships and silver in Asian Women's Championships. Becomes Pepsi MTV Youth Icon.
- 2009: Wins golds at Asian Indoor Games, AIBA Women's World Championships, Asian Women's Championships and is the recipient of the Rajiv Gandhi Khel Ratna Award.

- 2012: Wins gold at Asian Women's Championships and bronze at the London Olympics. Mary Kom becomes the first female Indian boxer to qualify for the Olympics and win a medal.
- 2013: Recipient of the Padma Bhushan Award.
- 2014: Bollywood movie on Mary Kom starring Priyanka Chopra releases to record the highest opening weekend of all time for a female-led film.
- 2016: Mary Kom is nominated as an honourable member of the Rajya Sabha by the President of India.
- 2018: Winner of golds at Asian Games, Asian Women's Championships, Commonwealth Games, and AIBA Women's World Championships. The Manipur government

honours Mary Kom with the prestigious title of 'Meethoi Leima' (exceptional or greatest lady).

- 2020: Recipient of the Padma Vibhushan Award.

# *Author's Note*

Two early incidents in my life introduced me to the world of boxing. My maternal uncle Chinmoy Mukherjee, who was in the Indian Air Force, was a huge fan of boxing and was always glued to the television whenever a boxing match was on. I remember accompanying him and my father, the late R.G. Ganguly, to witness my first live boxing match when I was a kid growing up in Jamshedpur. I was more fascinated at that impressionable age by how the colour of the shorts matched the colour of the boxer's gloves.

That local match introduced me to the world of boxing and I was literally hooked even though I was rooting for a knockout punch which unfortunately did not happen.

The second incident was reading the autobiography of arguably the best boxer in the world and certainly my favourite—Muhammad Ali. During my teenage years, my favourite chant during those occasional street fights (very rare I assure you) was 'I float like a butterfly. I swing like a bee. I am the greatest, I'm Swayam Ganguly.' Muhammad Ali ensured that I became a boxing fan for life and when the opportunity to write this biography of Mary Kom presented itself, thanks to Sudeshna Shome Ghosh, I literally grabbed it with both gloves. Sudeshna also deserves credit for editing the book so perfectly. Thank you to

Mohit Suneja for the superb illustrations in the book and also on the cover.

I would like to thank Mary Kom as reading her autobiography was not only insightful but also a delight. Digging the archives of newspapers like the *Times of India*, *Telegraph*, *Hindu*, *Deccan Herald*, *Imphal Times*, and *Imphal Free Press* aided the research process considerably.

This book is a dedication to my father R.G. Ganguly and the sheer resilience, talent, dedication and spirit of Mary Kom from a true fan of Indian boxing. As the great Muhammad Ali would have probably said, 'She floats like a butterfly, she stings like a bee. She is Mary Kom-BOMAYE!'

## HAVE YOU READ ALL THE *INCREDIBLE LIVES* BOOKS?

### *The Incredible Life of Milkha Singh: The Runner Who Could Fly*

He was an athlete who overcame life's odds to become one of India's greatest sporstpersons. This is his inspiring story of grit and determination.

In a small village in Punjab, little Milkha Singh grew up, loved by his parents, surrounded by open fields where he could run, play, and fly kites. In the heat of summer, when he had to walk to school barefoot, he would run like the wind so he could get home fast. And then, one day, in the midst of terrible violence and upheaval, his family and home were snatched away forever. Milkha, still a teenager, found himself alone and friendless, till he was recruited into the Army. Here, he finally found his passion and joy—running.

### *The Incredible Life of Jhalkari Bai: The Braveheart Warrior*

She was the bravest girl in her village. And one day, she became one of the bravest women her country had ever known.

Jhalkari Bai grew up in Bhojla, many miles away from the city of Jhansi. Far from the grand forts and palaces and illustrious kings and queens of Jhansi, in her village, she was known for her great strength and bravery—fighting off tigers and dacoits all alone. She nurtured a fierce desire to be a soldier, and to do amazing acts of courage. Today, Jhalkari Bai is present as just a footnote in history. But she lives on in the hearts of her people in Jhansi, Bhojla and beyond. This is her incredible and memorable story of bravery and sacrifice.

### *The Incredible Life of Birsa Munda: The Great Revolutionary*

He was a simple Adivasi boy. But one day he had to stand up and protest all the wrongs being done to his people. And so an unforgettable revolutionary was born.

Birsa Munda lived in one of the villages that dotted the Chhotanagpur region in today's Jharkhand. He was a dreamy boy with an uncanny ability to mesmerise not only humans but birds and animals too with his words and music. As he grew up, he became more and more aware of the exploitation of the Adivasi people by rich landowners and the British government. Birsa spoke out one day, and from that moment on, he started a journey that saw him become one of India's greatest tribal leaders and icons of resistance.

### *The Incredible Life of Savitribai Phule: The Fearless Reformer*

All she wanted was to be able to go to school. But she and many like her were denied this because of their caste. That did not stop her.

When she was nine years old, Savitri was married to thirteen-year-old Jyotirao Phule. Savitri yearned to be able to go to school, to read books. Jyotiba wanted his wife to be educated as well, and so he taught her. Soon, she learnt not just to read and write, but also trained as a teacher. Together, Savitribai and Jyotirao Phule started schools where girls and boys, dalit children, and those who had been shunned from schools till then could get educated. They fought against caste atrocities. They made sure that women learnt of their rights to exist with dignity.

*The Incredible Life of Bhagat Singh: The Indomitable Freedom Fighter*

He had a burning desire to see India as an independent country. He would stop at nothing to make it happen.

Born in 1907 to a family of farmers in Punjab, Bhagat Singh at the age of three had declared that he was sowing guns so he could fight the British colonisers. As he grew up, Bhagat Singh became a widely read and fiercely intelligent man. He would dedicate his life to not only making India free but also towards creating a more equitable society.

*The Incredible Life of Arati Saha: The Swimmer Who Wouldn't Give Up*

From the moment she learnt to swim, Arati set her eyes on difficult challenges. Then she decided to do what no Asian woman had done before—swim the English Channel.

Arati Saha was born in 1940, and learnt to swim in the Hooghly river in Calcutta as a child. At the age of eight, she competed in the National Championship in Bombay, winning silver and bronze medals. In 1952, she was selected as one of the first four women to represent independent India at the Helsinki Summer Olympics. At eleven years and ten months she was the youngest Indian Olympian—a record that stands till this day. By the time she was eighteen, Arati was looking for a fresh challenge—she decided to swim the English Channel.

*The Incredible Life of Anandibai Joshee: The Girl Who Fought to Be a Doctor*

Little Anandi was a strong and intelligent girl. Faced with tragedy as a child bride, she was determined to study to be a doctor and save lives.

Anandi led a very different life from other girls of the times. Her husband wanted her to study and made sure she could attend school. At the age of twelve, faced with a terrible loss, Anandi decided to become a doctor so she could help others. And she wanted to do so by going to faraway United States.